38,710

W9-BPJ-416

LIBRARY
EDWARD LITTLE HIGH SCHOOL

38,710

Egyptian
Islamic Jihad

Tamra Orr

The Rosen Publishing Group, Inc.
New York

LIBRARY
EDWARD LITTLE HIGH SCHOOL

*With compassion and empathy from within our family
to our entire world*

Published in 2003 by The Rosen Publishing Group, Inc.
29 East 21st Street, New York, NY 10010

Copyright © 2003 by The Rosen Publishing Group, Inc.

First Edition

All rights reserved. No part of this book may be reproduced in any form without permission in writing from the publisher, except by a reviewer.

Library of Congress Cataloging-in-Publication Data

Orr, Tamra.
Egyptian Islamic Jihad / Tamra Orr. — 1st ed.
    p. cm. — (Inside the world's most infamous terrorist organizations)
Summary: Discusses the origins, philosophy, and most notorious attacks of the Egyptian Islamic Jihad terrorist group, including their present activities, possible plans, and counter-terrorism efforts directed against them.
Includes bibliographical references and index.
ISBN 0-8239-3819-0 (lib. bdg.)
1. Tanzim al-Jihad al-Islami (Organization) 2. Islamic fundamentalism—Egypt. 3. Terrorists—Egypt. 4. Egypt—Politics and government—1970– . [1. Egyptian Islamic Jihad. 2. Terrorism. 3. Terrorists. 4. Islamic Fundamentalism.]
I. Title. II. series.
HV6433.E32T35 2002
962.05'5—dc21

200212829

Manufactured in the United States of America

Contents

LIBRARY
EDWARD LITTLE HIGH SCHOOL

Introduction

September 11, 2001, is a day that those who witnessed it will remember for the rest of their lives. On that dark day, three passenger planes, hijacked by members of Al Qaeda (a radical Islamic terrorist group led by Osama bin Laden), were turned into weapons of mass destruction as they were flown directly into prominent targets in the Washington, D.C., area and New York City. A fourth plane, possibly destined for the White House or Capitol, crashed in a field in Pennsylvania during a struggle between passengers and terrorists.

Older Americans watched in horror as the twin towers of New York's World Trade Center crumbled and part of the Pentagon in Virginia collapsed, knowing in their hearts that war had just been declared once more in their lifetime. Younger Americans watched in shock and fear as the images of airplanes careening into buildings were replayed on television over and over again. Never having experienced a foreign attack of such magnitude on American soil, they suddenly realized that the United States was far more vulnerable than they had previously thought.

Almost 3,000 people, from airplane passengers to police officers, office workers to firefighters, were killed in one single catastrophic day. The terrorists killed indiscriminately—rich and poor, American and foreign, Christian, Jewish, Hindu, Muslim, and atheist alike. Civilians from the United States and eighty other nations died,

United States president George W. Bush, accompanied by First Lady Laura Bush, speaks on December 11, 2001, during a White House ceremony commemorating the three-month anniversary of the September 11 attacks. Families of victims and police officers, firefighters, and other workers involved in the rescue efforts were present in the audience. More than seventy countries that lost citizens in the terrorist attacks also organized memorials and played their national anthems in tribute to the victims.

including dozens of Pakistanis, more than 130 Israelis, 250 Indians, as well as people from El Salvador, Iran, Mexico, Japan, and Britain.

After the shock and horror began to pass, these feelings were replaced by extreme grief, devastation, rage, and, finally, an even more powerful force—unity. In the troubled days following

Brennan Basnicki *(standing, left)* and Erica Basnicki *(standing, right)* are embraced by Father Thomas Rosica in St. Peter's Square, at the Vatican on March 21, 2002. The Canadian brother and sister lost their father, Ken, in the September 11 terrorist attacks on the World Trade Center. The Basnickis had just read a statement about their father's death in the presence of Pope John Paul II, who later embraced them and offered them words of comfort.

September 11, countries around the globe expressed their sorrow and banded together in support of the United States. The United States's national anthem could be heard playing on the streets of Paris, at Britain's Buckingham Palace, and at Berlin's Brandenburg Gate as each nation rallied around the United States. Moments of silence for the day's victims were observed throughout the world.

Along with the world's collective grief and anger came an urgent desire to learn the identities of the culprits. Who had masterminded this cruel attack against the United States? What country or group despised the United States so much that it would sacrifice its own people in order to make its hatred felt? Within hours of the attacks, the answers began to emerge. The growing amount of evidence seemed to indicate the involvement of Osama bin Laden and his Al Qaeda terrorist network. President George W. Bush proclaimed on September 20, 2001, the country's new "war on terrorism." In a nationally televised speech, President Bush abandoned the usually polite language of international diplomacy. He pulled no punches in characterizing the group as a pack of murderous terrorists:

> Al Qaeda is to terror what the Mafia is to crime. But its goal is not making money; its goal is remaking the world and imposing its radical beliefs on people everywhere. The terrorists practice a fringe form of Islamic extremism that has been rejected by Muslim scholars and the vast majority of Muslim clerics; a fringe movement that perverts the peaceful teachings of Islam . . . The terrorists' directive commands them to kill Christians and Jews, to kill all Americans and make no distinctions among military and civilians, including women and children. This group and its leader, a person named Osama bin Laden, are linked to many other organizations in different countries, including the Egyptian Islamic Jihad.

Because bin Laden became the focal point for the public's rage in the days following the September 11 attacks, the reference to the terrorist group Egyptian Islamic Jihad in Bush's speech went unnoticed by most Americans, yet it is a group that the country would be very unwise to ignore. It has a long history of killing and an increasingly close alliance with Al Qaeda.

Egyptian Islamic Jihad (which is distinct from the Palestinian terrorist group called simply Islamic Jihad) goes by a half dozen different names, including the Islamic Group, Al-Jihad al-Islami, the Jihad Group, and the Vanguards of Conquest. The militant Islamic organization's involvement in the deadliest act of terrorism committed against the United States is virtually beyond doubt. Sitting at Osama bin Laden's side throughout the years—and on September 11, 2001—was Ayman al-Zawahiri. He is the leader of Egyptian Islamic Jihad and the individual many believe to be the mastermind behind the entire September 11 attack.

Islamic Jihad has been merged with Al Qaeda since early 1998. It was the influence of al-Zawahiri and his followers that researchers believe led bin Laden to plan and carry out the attacks on the World Trade Center and the Pentagon. While Osama bin Laden is considered by Americans to be the most wanted man in the world, al-Zawahiri is right behind him, in position number two. He, along with the rest of the Islamic Jihad group, has been behind some of the most horrific terrorist acts of the last two decades. Together, they have engineered numerous assassinations and bombings that have killed thousands of people, most of them innocent civilians. In its turbulent wake, Egyptian Islamic Jihad never fails to leave behind a legacy of pain, wrath, and bloodshed.

The Birth of the Radical Islamists

Before anyone can understand what motivates the actions of the members of Egyptian Islamic Jihad, the basic tenets of Islam itself must be understood. Muslims are no more violent than any other group of people, but, like every human community, the Islamic world contains a small minority of extremist and violent members. Many Islamic nations and individual Muslims around the world expressed heartfelt outrage and sorrow over the September 11 attacks.

The Idea of Jihad

The five Pillars of Islam, around which Muslims are supposed to structure their lives, are: *shahadah*, or profession of faith in Allah (God); *salat*, or worship; *zakat*, or charity to the poor and needy; *sawm*, or a period of fasting; and *hajj*, or a pilgrimage to Mecca. The Islamists, as moderate Muslims call the extremists, want to add a sixth pillar—jihad. Jihad is a concept that is often misunderstood. The word "jihad" does not mean "holy war," as many often believe. It means a striving or a struggling to find and follow the way of Allah. The greater jihad is usually an internal struggle—the attempt to understand and do what is right and good. The lesser jihad is the fight to protect the Islamic faith and way of life. It is in this regard that Islamists are judged to go too far by many

CHAPTER

Young Pakistani students recite verses from the Koran at a *madrassa*, or Islamic school, outside the Pakistan capital, Islamabad. Many people think these schools teach Islamic militancy, extremism, and hatred rather than provide a religious education. Anywhere from 7,000 to 15,000 madrassas operate in Pakistan, serving several million students.

Muslim clerics (religious leaders and interpreters of the Islamic holy scripture, the Koran).

Radical Islamic terrorists often align themselves with fundamentalist clerics (extremely conservative religious leaders who promote a harsh version of Islam). These clerics, perceived as holy by their followers, issue strict interpretations of the Koran. They view the call to jihad as permission to use violence and murder as a means of keeping the faith safe. According to this interpretation of the Koran, killing a non-Muslim is not murder; rather, it is holy and nonpunishable. Any infidel, or unbeliever, is viewed as a threat to the Islamic faith. Since Islamists see Western culture—particularly the global influence of the United States—as a threat to their faith, they think they have divine permission to kill anyone from these non-Islamic countries.

Islamists do not believe in the separation of church and state, in which people are free to practice any faith that they choose—including no faith whatsoever—without government interference. Instead, Islamists demand that their society be ruled by clerics and governed by religious law. Every aspect of citizens' lives—from their public duties to their private entertainment—would be determined by the clerics' harsh interpretations of the Koran's moral principles.

Some Islamists will do whatever they feel is necessary to install a conservative Muslim regime, to promote their agenda, and to terrorize their perceived enemies, including assassinations, hostage-takings, hijackings, and bombings of public places. Needless to say, most Muslims find these actions repulsive and want no part of them. Nahid Awad, executive director of CAIR, the Council on American–Islamic Relations, was quoted as saying, "There is no place in Islam for acts of terrorism and violence

Militant Islamists hold copies of the Koran as they shout anti-Israeli and anti-American slogans during a protest rally in Amman, Jordan, on March 16, 2002. The demonstration, which attracted thousands of Jordanian marchers, was organized to show support for the Palestinian uprising against Israeli occupation of the West Bank and Gaza Strip, territory Palestinians consider to be their own.

against innocent people." Instead, he commented that the "true face of the community" could be found in the New York Muslim firefighters aiding in the World Trade Center rescue efforts, as well as the Muslim doctors treating the victims of September 11 and Muslim volunteers donating blood. After all, Awad was quoted by CNN.com as saying at a news conference, "We all came on different ships, but we are all in the same boat."

The Muslim Brotherhood

One of the first modern militant Islamic groups was the Muslim Brotherhood, formed in Egypt in 1928 as an Islamic revivalist society. Its motto was, "Allah is our objective. The Prophet is our leader. Qur'an [Koran] is our law. Jihad is our way. Dying in the way of Allah is our highest hope."

The founder of the group was a man named Hassan al-Banna, a twenty-two-year-old elementary school teacher. He was living in turbulent times. The Ottoman Empire, a religious regime based in what is modern-day Turkey, lasted from the fourteenth century to 1922, when the Turkish republic was established by Mustafa Kemal, or Atatürk (Father of the Turks) as he was later named. Throughout the almost 500-year history of the empire, Muslims were united under a single ruler and began to extend their influence as never before. The Ottoman Empire controlled much of the Middle East and even gained a foothold in Europe, establishing Islamic traditions and culture there that remain to this day (the Muslims in Bosnia and Bulgaria are the last descendants of the Ottoman presence in Europe).

With the establishment of the Turkish republic, Atatürk began secularizing Turkish society (making it less dominated by religion). This shocked al-Banna and others who felt that they and their faith

In 1923, Mustafa Kemal (1881–1938), who later referred to himself as Atatürk (Father of the Turks), declared himself president of the new Turkish republic following the end of the Ottoman Empire (a Muslim regime that ruled parts of Europe, Asia Minor, and the Middle East for almost 500 years). The social, cultural, and political changes he introduced were radical and immediate. Western penal codes (the classification of crimes and system of punishments) were adopted. The Roman alphabet replaced Arabic script. Even traditional dress was forcibly abandoned in favor of Western fashions. Atatürk himself read, wrote, and spoke French.

were being betrayed. In response, they formed the Muslim Brotherhood in Egypt in 1928. They believed that Islam, in addition to being a religion, was an all-encompassing way of life that should infuse and dictate politics, education, social customs, leisure activities, and private life. To them, faith in Islam demanded a commitment to a certain way of living, a commitment that was impossible to make in a secular society.

For more than two decades, the Muslim Brotherhood grew steadily. As their numbers swelled, so did their anger. One particular provocation was the establishment of the state of Israel on May 14, 1948, on what most Muslims considered sacred Arab land. Feeling that Egypt was not taking a strong enough stand against Israel or launching a sufficiently powerful defense of the Palestinians, the Muslim Brotherhood began to perform terrorist attacks in Egypt, where the movement was declared illegal. Despite the ban, the Muslim Brotherhood managed to assassinate the prime minister of Egypt, Mahmud Fahmi Nokrashi, on December 28, 1948. In retaliation, Egyptian government agents assassinated al-Banna in Cairo in February 1949.

The Egyptian government allowed the Muslim Brotherhood to operate as a religious organization, but not as a political party. In 1954, however, all group activities were banned after the Brotherhood insisted that Egypt be governed under *sharia*, or Islamic law. That same year, a member of the group, Abdul Munim Abdul Rauf, attempted to assassinate Egyptian president Gamal Abdul Nasser. Though the attempt failed, Rauf was executed along with five other group members. More than 4,000 additional members of the Brotherhood were arrested, while thousands of others fled to Syria, Saudi Arabia, Jordan, and Lebanon.

Hoping to dilute interest in a new political party that had formed to challenge his rule—the Arab Socialist Union—Nasser offered amnesty (a pardon that grants prisoners their freedom) to the imprisoned Muslim Brotherhood members in 1964. The Muslim extremists rewarded Nasser's gesture of reconciliation with three more attempts on his life. As a result, in 1966, the top leaders of the group were executed and many rank-and-file members were again imprisoned.

Despite the fact that the Muslim Brotherhood is now illegal in Egypt, its members were still able to obtain seventeen seats in the Egyptian parliament in the 2000 elections, running as independents. In addition, many Brotherhood members hold important offices in a variety of professional organizations throughout Egypt. In recent years, the group has tried to gain greater political legitimacy and seems to have no ties to any active radical Egyptian Islamic groups.

The Birth of Egyptian Islamic Jihad

By the early 1970s, radical Islamists were looking to form a new group, since the Muslim Brotherhood had become so weakened through executions and imprisonments. Following Egyptian president Anwar Sadat's release of most Islamic prisoners in 1971, several groups of militants began to form and became loosely allied. These included the Islamic Liberation Party, al-Takfir wal-Hijra (Arabic for "Excommunication and Emigration"), Al Najun min-al-nar ("Saved from the Inferno"), Al-Gama'a al-Islamiyya ("The Islamic Group"), and Al-Jihad ("Holy War").

All of these groups were influenced by the militant ideology of Sayyid Qutb, an Islamic activist who was executed by the Egyptian government in 1966. Qutb felt that Arab secular governments betray the Islamic faith, and therefore must be violently overthrown. He had preached that all Muslim states should be ruled by the Koran; otherwise they violated religious law and jihad must be declared against them. The members of the new Islamist groups that Qutb inspired felt that government ministers and officials, police officers, liberal and secular Arab intellectuals, Coptic Christians (an ancient Egyptian branch of Christianity), and tourists were legitimate targets during jihad.

Egyptian Islamic Jihad at a Glance

- Active since the late 1970s.

- Currently divided into two factions: Al-Jihad (led by Dr. Ayman al-Zawahiri and united in 1998 with Osama bin Laden's Al Qaeda terrorist network) and the Vanguards of Conquest (led by Ahmad Husayn Agiza).

- The group's spiritual leader is Sheikh Omar Abd al-Rahman, imprisoned in the United States for conspiracy to bomb the World Trade Center and other New York landmarks.

- Egyptian Islamic Jihad operates in small, secretive cells (groups of two or three terrorists) and recruits members aged fifteen to thirty. Its members are trained in remote camps in Egypt, Afghanistan, Pakistan, Sudan, and elsewhere.

- The group receives funding from Iran, Sudan, and Osama bin Laden. It also raises money among prominent and sympathetic Egyptians, Islamic institutions, and groups that pose as legitimate Islamic charities and relief organizations.

- Egyptian Islamic Jihad has claimed responsibility for numerous terrorist attacks against Egyptian government officials and institutions, Christian leaders and institutions, and Israeli and Western targets in Egypt.

- The group's mission is to establish Islamic rule in Egypt by force and attack anyone or anything that represents secularism (the exclusion of religion) or Western influences. Following its 1998 alliance with Al Qaeda, the group's goals now encompass a more general attack upon American targets worldwide.

The Birth of the Radical Islamists

By the late 1970s, one of these groups in particular, Egyptian Islamic Jihad, often referred to as Al-Jihad, was growing strong. Initially, its members were drawn mainly from Egyptian jails. Later, students and professors from the country's universities who were familiar with the teachings of the radical Islamists began joining as well. Like the other groups inspired by Sayyid Qutb's ideas, Egyptian Islamic Jihad's main goal is to overthrow Egypt's secular government and to replace it with an Islamic state. Beyond that, it is also committed to destroying any secular establishment—including the governments of other Arab nations—that is perceived to represent a threat to Islam. Finally, it seeks to attack U.S. and Israeli interests in Egypt and abroad.

One of Egyptian Islamic Jihad's first actions was also one of its most infamous and shocking: the assassination of Egyptian president and 1978 Nobel Peace Prize winner Anwar Sadat. Jihad members, enflamed by the teachings of their spiritual leader, the radical cleric Omar Abd al-Rahman, had been furious with Sadat ever since his participation in the 1977 Camp David Summit. During these meetings between Sadat and Israeli prime minister Menachem Begin, U.S. president Jimmy Carter had helped to negotiate a peace agreement between Israel and Egypt. Jihad members felt it was the greatest betrayal of Islam so far, especially since, as part of the agreement, Sadat officially recognized Israel's right to exist, something no other Middle Eastern Arab leader had done. He came to be viewed by many Islamists as a traitor to the Arab world and an American and Israeli pawn.

Sadat's search for peace in the Middle East required tremendous political and personal courage. Sadly, his act of bravery also sealed his fate.

Egyptian
—Islamic Jihad's—
Bloody Debut

Soon after its formation, Egyptian Islamic Jihad quickly established a reputation for the targeting of high-profile government leaders. Because these officials served a secular regime, they were viewed as traitors to the Islamic faith by Al-Jihad members. The group's first attack on the Egyptian government would also prove to be one of its most shocking: the 1981 assassination of Anwar Sadat.

The Violent Death of a Peacemaker

Egypt in August 1981 was not a pleasant place to be. The summer was unusually hot, and the water supply was limited. Fighting erupted between Muslims and Coptic Christians in a slum area of Cairo, and many people were killed, including children. The Muslims blamed the Christians; the Christians blamed the Muslims. By September, an exasperated Sadat began to put pressure on both groups to stop the fighting. Finally, he had more than 1,600 people arrested, Islamic student groups were banned, and Pope Shenouda III (the patriarch of the Coptic Christian Church) was banished to a monastery.

Many Egyptians were angry. Though Sadat had won the Nobel Peace Prize for his participation in the Camp David Accords that created peace with Israel, the average Egyptian's life remained unchanged. Poverty and political repression were still the lot of

Egyptian president Anwar Sadat at an annual military review parade minutes before he was assassinated by Islamic militants associated with Egyptian Islamic Jihad on October 6, 1981. As Sadat saluted the troops marching past him, several Muslim fundamentalist soldiers, led by First Lieutenant Khalid al-Islambouli, ran from one of the vehicles in the parade and began firing machine guns and throwing grenades into Sadat's reviewing stand. Sadat was killed, and twenty others, including four American diplomats, were injured.

most Egyptians. Sadat's reaction to social and political turmoil of this kind was usually mass arrests and censorship, which only further inflamed the anger of the Egyptian people, particularly the Islamists. One of the people arrested by Sadat was Sheikh Abd al-Hamid Kishk, a popular and influential preacher who angered

Onlookers take cover in the reviewing stand following the assassi-nation of Egyptian president Anwar Sadat on October 6, 1981, dur-ing an annual military parade. Among those in the reviewing stand who escaped injury were future UN secretary-general Boutros Boutros-Ghali and future Egyptian president Hosni Mubarak (who was then Sadat's vice president). Mubarak was sitting just to the right of Sadat, yet somehow avoided serious injury.

the president by demanding that Cairo's al-Azhar Mosque operate free of government control. This demand was interpreted as a call for the overthrow of the government, and Kishk was arrested and put in jail. He, along with Omar Abd al-Rahman, the blind religious scholar who would come to be considered the spiritual leader of Egyptian Islamic Jihad, encouraged militant radicals to actively oppose the government and its actions.

During an annual military parade on October 6, 1981, members of Islamic Jihad, who were serving in the Egyptian army, hijacked a military truck and joined the parade. While Sadat was reviewing and saluting the troops, the group members jumped from the truck and began to fire weapons and throw hand grenades in the president's direction. Army first lieutenant and Jihad member Khalid al-Islambouli shot Sadat and yelled, "I am Khalid al-Islambouli! I have killed Pharaoh!" Sadat was killed and twenty others were hurt, including four American diplomats. Al-Islambouli and four others were executed for their role in the assassination.

Assassination attempts did not end there, however. In 1993, Egyptian Islamic Jihad attempted to assassinate the Egyptian interior minister Hassan al-Alfi. He was injured when a bomb packed with ball bearings exploded near his car. Al-Alfi escaped with his life, but five others died. In that same year, the group tried unsuccessfully to assassinate Egyptian prime minister Atef Sedky with a car bomb. One innocent bystander was killed and eighteen were injured.

Omar Abd al-Rahman

Omar Abd al-Rahman was born in 1938. As a young child, he was blinded by the disease diabetes. He went on to become a religious scholar whose conservative interpretations of the Koran and anti-Western attitudes made him a natural fit for the role of spiritual adviser to Egyptian Islamic Jihad.

In this position, he was able to write a 1981 fatwa (a religious command) that urged his followers to fight for their beliefs, no matter what the cost. This "holy war" could include the killing of Christians and stealing gold from Christian jewelry stores to finance the jihad. Al-Rahman felt that Americans and other Western tourists and officials in Egypt were a plague upon his country. These infidels (nonbelievers) had to be removed from Muslim lands in any way possible. The cleric viewed Egyptians who sought closer ties to the West as traitors and enemies of Islam who must be punished accordingly.

The intentionally vague wording of al-Rahman's fatwa gave many extremists the freedom to do whatever they felt was necessary in defense of Islam—including killing innocent people. It is believed that it was al-Rahman's words that inspired Egyptian Islamic Jihad to assassinate Sadat. Indeed, al-Rahman was considered to be an accessory (someone who contributes to a crime but is not the main perpetrator) in that murder because of his fiery writing, and he was arrested. His exact role in the assassination and his relationship to Egyptian Islamic Jihad remained vague, however, and al-Rahman was acquitted (set free with charges dropped) in 1984.

Although cleared of the charges against him and set free, al-Rahman was added to the United States's official list of terrorists. Despite this, however, he was able to sneak into the United States in 1990. He became the head of a mosque in Jersey City, New Jersey, where he and a group of coconspirators began to plan their next attack in the name of Islam. This time, however, the location would not be Egypt. The spiritual leader of Egyptian Islamic Jihad and his followers would now wage their holy war on American soil.

The 1993 World Trade Center Attack

The followers of Sheikh Omar Abd al-Rahman, Egyptian Islamic Jihad's spiritual leader, broadened their base of operations and range of targets. No longer confining themselves to attacks on Egyptian officials and foreign tourists, they were now planning to take their anti-Western jihad to American shores, viewed as the very source of the evil influences that threatened Islam. Plans got underway for an all new type of terrorist act—one committed on American soil, against innocent people. Al-Rahman's new strategy would serve as an eerie prelude to the attacks of September 11 and would send a clear signal of Islamic hostility to which the United States may not have paid careful enough heed.

At 12:18 PM on February 26, 1993, there was a huge explosion on the second level of the underground parking garage of New York's World Trade Center. Hidden in the rear cargo area of a Ford F350 Econoline van, rented, driven, and parked by followers of al-Rahman, were 1,100 pounds (499 kilograms) of the homemade, fertilizer-based explosive urea nitrate. Underneath that were three large, metal cylinders of compressed and highly combustible hydrogen gas. Six people were killed and more than a thousand were injured by the explosion. The other 50,000 were safely evacuated from the towers.

When the dust had settled, property damage estimates were placed at more than a half billion dollars. The explosion created a crater 150 feet in diameter and five floors deep. Despite the extent of the devastation below the Trade Center, the structure of the towers was soon declared undamaged and sound, a testament to the buildings' strength and engineering genius. Up to

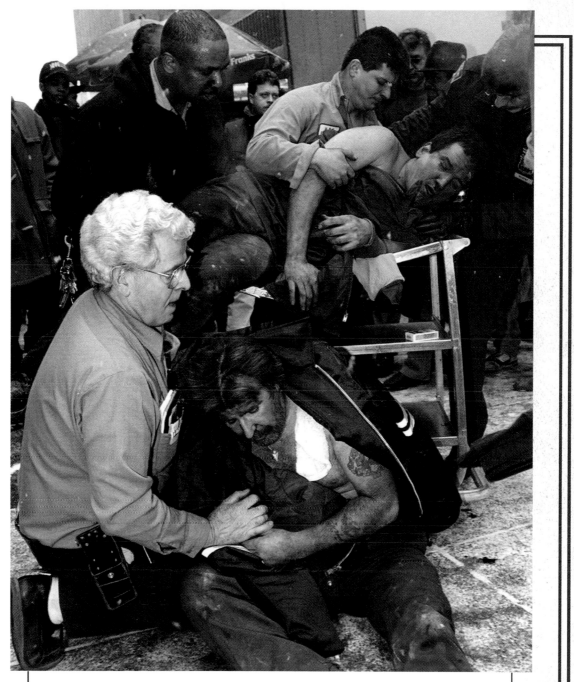

Victims of the February 26, 1993, terrorist bomb explosion at the World Trade Center in New York City receive assistance from rescue personnel and others. Four principal suspects associated with Sheikh Omar Abd al-Rahman, the spiritual leader of Egyptian Islamic Jihad, were quickly arrested, convicted, and each sentenced to 240 years in prison.

that time in U.S. history, this attack was the most significant international terrorist act ever committed on American soil. It created the largest crime scene in New York history up to that point and was called the "case of the century." Little did the city and the country know that this was just a preview of the scene of unimaginable devastation that was to come eight and a half years later, at the dawn of the next century.

The Investigation

There were many dangers posed by structural damage in the Trade Center's parking garage. These included ruptured sewage lines, exposure to asbestos, the leaking of acid and fuel from destroyed cars, and the falling of sharp metal and chunks of concrete. Yet members of the Joint Terrorism Task Force (a law enforcement group made up of FBI agents and New York Police Department officers) were still able to comb the area for information and clues. In all the tangled and charred debris, they somehow discovered a piece of the van's frame. Incredibly, the vehicle's serial number etched upon it was still visible.

This serial number provided the first clue in a chain of evidence that led the United States to the four main suspects who were quickly arrested: Mohammed Salameh, Nidal Ayyad, Mahmud Abouhalima, and Ahmad M. Ajaj. The trial lasted six months, and the prosecuting attorneys brought forth more than 200 witnesses and 1,000 exhibits. The picture that emerged of the terrorists' intent was chilling. For instance, it is thought that the terrorists were planning to topple the north tower of the World Trade Center into the south tower while releasing a cloud of cyanide gas into the air. Luckily, the heat of the van's explosion burned off the gas, and the towers managed to withstand the brutal explosion relatively unharmed.

In the end, all four suspects were found guilty on thirty-eight different counts and sent to prison. The mastermind of the entire operation, Ahmed Ramzi Yousef, an engineer and bomb expert, was born in either Kuwait, Iraq, Pakistan, or the United Arab Emirates. He was not permanently linked to any one terrorist group, but instead seemed to lend his services and expertise to a number of radical Islamic groups. Yousef fled to the Philippines following the attack. While attempting to mix chemical explosives for use in a bomb, Yousef accidentally started a fire and fled his apartment, which was soon raided by the police.

There they found evidence of a plot Yousef and his associates had devised to blow up eleven commercial transpacific airplanes that originated in the United States. The eleven explosions were to occur in a single day, within minutes of each other. Yousef had successfully attempted a "dry run" in 1994 when he bombed a Philippine Airlines plane, killing one passenger. The pilot managed to land the plane safely. He was also linked to unsuccessful plots to assassinate Pope John Paul II and U.S. president Bill Clinton. It is thought that these three unfulfilled plots may have been set in motion on Osama bin Laden's orders.

Yousef would not be caught until 1995 in Pakistan. He was convicted in 1996 in New York for his role in the World Trade Center bombing. Yousef's partner in the planning of the bombing, Abdul Rahman Yasin, an American citizen born in Bloomington, Indiana, also fled the country after the 1993 attack. He is still at large and wanted by the authorities. A $5,000,000 reward has been offered for information leading to his capture.

Who's Who in Egyptian Islamic Jihad

Mahmud Abouhalima: The active ringleader of the 1993 World Trade Center bombing; drove the getaway car and received 240 years in prison.

Ahmad Husayn Agiza: Leader of the Vanguards of Conquest, a faction of Egyptian Islamic Jihad.

Mohammed Atta: Thirty-three-year-old architect and member of Egyptian Islamic Jihad who was allegedly at the controls of American Airlines Flight 11 when it struck the north tower of the World Trade Center on September 11, 2001.

Dr. Abdullah Azzam: Palestinian Islamic activist who taught Osama bin Laden at King Abdulaziz University in Saudi Arabia. Founded the Jihad Service Bureau. Joined with bin Laden and al-Zawahiri to recruit and train Muslims for Al-Jihad.

Hasan al-Banna: Founder of the Muslim Brotherhood, one of the first militant Islamic groups, out of which Egyptian Islamic Jihad and many other Egyptian terrorist groups developed.

Khalid al-Islambouli: Organized and led mission to assassinate Egyptian president Anwar Sadat in October 1981; executed in April 1982.

Bashir Mousa: One of three founders of Egyptian Islamic Jihad in the late 1970s.

Abdul Aziz Odeh: One of three founders of Egyptian Islamic Jihad in the late 1970s

Mohammed Salameh: 1993 World Trade Center bomber arrested when he tried to collect the deposit on the van he had rented to carry the explosive materials.

Fathi Shikaki: Original leader of Egyptian Islamic Jihad until 1995; executed by Israeli agents.

Sheikh Omar Abd al-Rahman speaks during a press conference held six days before the February 26, 1993, bombing of the World Trade Center in New York City. Arrested three months after the attack, al-Rahman and nine other Islamic radicals were accused of taking part in the conspiracy to bomb the World Trade Center, as well as unfulfilled plans to attack other New York landmarks. In 1995, he and his codefendants, who included Sudanese, Egyptian, Jordanian, and American citizens, were convicted of conspiracy and related charges. Each received life in prison.

A New Kind of Terrorism

In June 1993, Sheikh Omar Abd al-Rahman was arrested after an undercover operation linked him to a plot to bomb other New York landmarks and transportation hubs, such as the Holland and Lincoln Tunnels, the George Washington Bridge, and the United

Nations building. In addition, plans to assassinate the then-U.S. senator from New York, Alfonse D'Amato, and the then-UN secretary-general, Boutros Boutros-Ghali, were uncovered. Boutros-Ghali was himself an Egyptian Coptic Christian and a close friend of Egyptian president Hosni Mubarak. Al-Rahman and nine other conspirators were charged in this plot and were also charged with conspiracy in the 1993 World Trade Center bombing. In October 1995, they were all convicted in New York and sentenced to life in prison. Though behind bars, al-Rahman continues to issue fatwas and to exert a powerful influence over the members of Egyptian Islamic Jihad. Group members still regard al-Rahman as their spiritual leader and an Islamic prophet, and their violence is undiminished.

In the wake of the 1993 World Trade Center bombing, many government officials, intelligence agents, and average citizens wondered whether this signaled the beginning of a new kind of global terrorism. Terrorists now seemed to be gathering in loosely organized groups of fundamentalists less concerned with promoting the interests of a particular country or specific group of people, and more interested in waging all-out religious and ideological war. Indeed, groups such as Egyptian Islamic Jihad, guided by the American-based Sheikh Omar Abd al-Rahman and assisted by terrorist mercenaries such as Ahmed Ramzi Yousef, were no longer simply protesting peace with Israel or fighting to rid Egypt of the "corrupting" Western culture. Instead, they now seemed to be seeking to rid the entire world of American influence by taking the fight right to the United States's doorstep.

Jihad's New
Leader

In the late 1980s, Egyptian Islamic Jihad became fragmented because of mass arrests by Egyptian security authorities. Eventually, the group split into two. The new faction calls itself the Vanguards of Conquest (Talaa' al-Fateh) and is led by Ahmad Husayn Agiza. The original Jihad group responsible for the assassination of Anwar Sadat is led by Dr. Ayman al-Zawahiri, an Egyptian physician. It remains unclear, however, just how separate these factions are, and some sources name al-Zawahiri as the leader of the Vanguards of Conquest. Al-Zawahiri's faction was based in Afghanistan until the launch of Operation Enduring Freedom—the United States-led military action designed to root out the terrorists responsible for the September 11 attacks put the group and its leader on the run after October 7, 2001.

Abdul al-Zumar, the former leader of Egyptian Islamic Jihad, is imprisoned in Egypt. He may be trying to steer the Al-Jihad movement in a less violent path, having issued a call for his followers to form a "peaceful front." The sincerity of this plea is uncertain, however, because it was issued together with Sheikh Omar Abd al-Rahman, a man who has rarely shown any inclination to embrace peaceful dialogue.

Under the leadership of al-Zawahiri, Egyptian Islamic Jihad would become more and more focused on attacking Western— primarily U.S.—interests around the world. By 1994, the group

3

had all but ceased attacking targets in Egypt. Instead, it turned its attention to the bombing of embassies throughout Asia, the Middle East, and Africa. Further radicalized by al-Zawahiri, Egyptian Islamic Jihad had embraced global jihad.

Ayman al-Zawahiri

Born on June 19, 1951, outside of Cairo, Ayman al-Zawahiri, like Osama bin Laden, was a child of privilege. He grew up in a prominent Egyptian family. One of his grandfathers was an ambassador and the other was an influential Muslim cleric; both were renowned scholars. His father was a prominent professor of pharmacology (the science of drugs and medicines), so al-Zawahiri's choice of a career in medicine was no surprise. Al-Zawahiri would eventually earn a master's degree in surgery and work as a pediatrician (a doctor who specializes in treating children).

Al-Zawahiri's family describes him as having been a quiet, studious, and deeply religious child who often wrote poetry to his mother. In his young adulthood, however, he underwent a transformation that eventually would place him at the head of one of the most violent terrorist organizations in history.

As a student in the 1960s, al-Zawahiri got caught up in the Islamic fundamentalist movements that were gripping Egypt at the time. He was only a teenager when he joined the Muslim Brotherhood and became an activist, eventually becoming a member of Islamic Jihad when it began to take shape in the late 1970s. He became well known enough to the authorities as a radical Islamist to get caught up in the police dragnet that followed the assassination of President Anwar Sadat. He was one of the 302 Egyptians arrested and tried on conspiracy charges for that murder. Acquitted of

Ayman al-Zawahiri is pictured here in a still image from a videotape broadcast by the Arabic satellite news channel Al Jazeera, on October 7, 2001. It was filmed in an undisclosed location in Afghanistan. On this same day, U.S. and British forces began their air attacks against Taliban and Al Qaeda forces in retaliation for the September 11, 2001, terrorist attacks upon the World Trade Center and the Pentagon. Al-Zawahiri is the leader of Egyptian Islamic Jihad and a close ally and confidant of Osama bin Laden. He is also thought to be the true mastermind and energizing force behind many of bin Laden's terrorist plots, including the September 11 attacks.

conspiracy, he was convicted on an unrelated weapons charge and spent three years in prison, where he was tortured.

Since he could speak fluent English, al-Zawahiri became a spokesperson for the other Islamists who were imprisoned. When he was released in 1985, he left Egypt and spent time in Saudi

Arabia, Pakistan, and Afghanistan. In the early 1990s, he traveled extensively in western Europe, living in both Switzerland and Denmark. In 1995, he even entered the United States and raised money for future Egyptian Islamic Jihad attacks. Wherever he traveled, he attempted to revive interest in Egyptian Islamic Jihad, a movement severely weakened in Egypt by mass arrests. By working to form international chapters of the group, al-Zawahiri was broadening the Jihad network and laying the groundwork for its new emphasis on attacks on Western interests outside Egypt.

Al-Zawahiri's interest in global jihad may have been sparked by a chance encounter he had in the mid-1980s in Afghanistan. Al-Zawahiri had traveled there to help treat the wounded Muslim fighters who were resisting the Soviet invasion of that country (which lasted from 1979 to 1989). While there, he met Osama bin Laden, who had funded and organized a group of Arab militants to help fight alongside Afghanistan's Muslim warriors. The two, who had very similar views on Islamic fundamentalism and radicalism, became close. This growing friendship would bear extremely bitter fruit in the years to come.

A New Direction

In the early 1990s, Egyptian Islamic Jihad appeared to be continuing its policy of launching attacks in Egypt against government authorities and individuals who they felt represented Western corruption and secularism. In 1992, Egyptian Islamic Jihad murdered Faraj Fodah, an author who had openly supported Israeli-Egyptian peace. Several unsuccessful assassination attempts included those on Interior Minister Hassan al-Alfi and Prime Minister Atef Sedky in 1993. An Egyptian Islamic Jihad hit list surfaced around this time and included the names of prominent Egyptians to be killed, including ministers and journalists. These assassination plots seemed to carry on the group's bloody tradition, first established by the murder of Anwar Sadat in 1981.

In reality, however, Egyptian Islamic Jihad, under the leadership of Dr. Ayman al-Zawahiri, was in the process of turning its deadly gaze outward. Having spent more than twenty years fighting the enemy within, al-Zawahiri was preparing to attack the enemies—U.S. citizens particularly—on their own turf.

Embassy Plots

Al-Zawahiri's travels through western Europe and the United States were intended at least in part to raise money for a series of embassy bombings that he was planning. The first plot involved the simultaneous bombing of the American and Israeli Embassies in Manila, the Philippines, a plan that was never carried out. It was thought to have been concocted by both al-Zawahiri and Osama bin Laden and is generally attributed to Al Qaeda.

Al-Zawahiri's next embassy plot would be put into action, however, and would achieve deadly results. On November 19, 1995, an Egyptian Islamic Jihad suicide bomber drove a vehicle loaded with explosives into the Egyptian Embassy in Islamabad, Pakistan. This embassy is believed to have been a key base for Egyptian intelligence operations against Islamic militants. Seventeen people were killed and sixty were hurt. The explosion destroyed the entire compound and inflicted structural damage to nearby buildings, such as the Japanese and Indonesian Embassies and a bank. Shattered glass and debris stretched out over a half-mile radius. Following this attack, al-Zawahiri would be sentenced to death in

A large crater in front of the Egyptian Embassy in Islamabad, Pakistan, created by an explosion on November 19, 1995. An Egyptian Islamic Jihad suicide bomber drove a pickup truck packed with explosives into the gate of the embassy, killing seventeen people and wounding sixty others. Ayman al-Zawahiri was widely suspected of masterminding the attack upon the embassy, a key base for Egyptian intelligence operations against Islamic militants. He was quickly sentenced to death in absentia by an Egyptian military court for his activities with Egyptian Islamic Jihad.

Massacre at Luxor

While Egyptian Islamic Jihad began to attack American targets outside of Egypt, its ally, Al-Gama'a al-Islamiyya, continued to wage its jihad at home. Under the spiritual direction of Sheikh Omar Abd al-Rahman and sometimes receiving instructions from al-Zawahiri, the group was responsible for many attacks upon tourists throughout the 1990s, including attacks upon tour buses, trains, hotels, and cruise ships. Its biggest attack, however, occurred in the shadow of Egypt's pyramids and is believed to have been organized by al-Zawahiri.

Three hundred miles south of Cairo is the temple site of Luxor where visitors from many countries come to see the tombs of pharaohs. On the morning of November 17, 1997, busloads of tourists were lining up to see the sites when members of Al-Gama'a al-Islamiyya jumped out of a hijacked bus and began shooting. In just a few frantic moments, sixty-seven foreign tourists were killed and another twenty-six injured. The dead included thirty-four Swiss tourists, eight Japanese, five Germans, four British, and individuals from several other countries.

absentia (without being present) by an Egyptian military court for his activities with Egyptian Islamic Jihad.

An even bigger embassy plot was looming on the horizon, however. It would introduce the world to a new and deadly alliance, one that would unite the two most dangerous masterminds of Islamic terrorism.

An Unholy Alliance

Osama bin Laden and Dr. Ayman al-Zawahiri first met in Afghanistan in the late 1980s during the last days of the successful fight to turn back the Soviet invasion of that Muslim country. They both came from wealthy families, but had turned their backs on luxury and privilege to help fund and organize some of the most destructive terrorist acts in the history of Islamic radicalism. In that first meeting, the two men discovered they shared a common vision of jihad and quickly became close friends.

A Partnership Forms Over Time

Following the Soviet withdrawal from Afghanistan in 1989, the two went their separate ways. Al-Zawahiri traveled widely, raising money in an attempt to transform Egyptian Islamic Jihad into a terrorist group that could operate on an international stage. Bin Laden set up his Al Qaeda base of operations first in Sudan and then in Afghanistan. In these locations, he set up a network of camps that trained Al Qaeda operatives and members of other radical Islamic groups in the techniques of terrorism. Upon completion of their training, these terrorists would fan out across the globe, form terrorist cells of three or four members, melt into the societies of their adopted homes, and await instructions for an attack.

Investigators in a speedboat examine the damaged hull of the USS *Cole* at the Yemeni port of Aden on October 15, 2000. Three days earlier, on October 12, a powerful explosion ripped a hole in the U.S. Navy destroyer, killing seventeen soldiers and injuring thirty-seven others. The port serves as one of the navy's refueling centers for ships involved in operations in the Persian Gulf. A pair of suicide bombers linked to Al Qaeda steered a small boat loaded with military-grade plastic explosives alongside the *Cole* as it was being refueled. The two stood at attention just before the explosion tore a sixty-foot-wide by forty-foot-high hole in the destroyer's hull.

Operating separately, Al Qaeda and Egyptian Islamic Jihad (or similar groups funded and directed by bin Laden and al-Zawahiri) realized their dream of global jihad. They reigned terror on American interests throughout the 1990s, bombing the World Trade Center and embassies, attacking U.S. military barracks in Saudi Arabia and the USS *Cole* in Yemen, and killing American peacekeepers in Sudan. At some point, bin Laden and al-Zawahiri must have realized that working together would achieve even more deadly results than their solo efforts had.

A Call to Murder

On February 23, 1998, al-Zawahiri and bin Laden announced the formation of a new group called the World Islamic Front for the Jihad Against the Jews and the Crusaders (Crusaders were medieval European Christians who sought to recapture Jerusalem and the biblical Holy Land from the Muslims). The group's goals include the removal of the United States's presence in Saudi Arabia, the end of the United Nations embargo against Iraq (a legacy of that country's invasion of its neighbor Kuwait), and the granting of Palestinian control over Muslim holy places in Jerusalem. The group is made up of seasoned Muslim militants and extremists ranging from Chechens to Saudis, Jordanians to Afghans.

In addition, bin Laden and al-Zawahiri issued a fatwa describing the killing of American civilians and military personnel as an "obligation for every Muslim." This decree was also signed by Abu-Yasser Rifai Ahmad Taha (of the Egyptian Islamic Group), Shaykh Mir Hamzah (secretary of a radical Islamic group, Jamiat-ul-Ulema-e-Pakistan), and Fazlur Rahman (an imprisoned Islamist spiritual leader).

The fatwa offers three justifications for violent attacks upon Americans:

1. The United States has been occupying Islamic lands and plundering its riches, dictating to its rulers, humiliating its people, terrorizing its neighbors, and waging war against the followers of Allah.

2. The United States is responsible for killing more than one million of the Iraqi people and is trying to destroy them altogether.

3. The United States wishes to pull apart all the states of the region, such as Saudi Arabia, Egypt, and Sudan, in order to support Israel's survival and distract attention from the murder of Palestinian Muslims there.

Because of these alleged crimes, the United States is viewed as having declared war on Allah, his prophet Muhammad, and all Muslim people. It is a solemn duty, therefore, of the Muslim people to defend their faith from these attacks. As the World Islamic Front statement says, "The ruling to kill the Americans and their allies—civilians and military—is an individual duty for every Muslim who can do it in any country in which it is possible to do it." Bin Laden is further quoted as saying, in an interview with ABC News in 1998, "In today's wars, there are no morals. We believe the worst thieves in the world today and the worst terrorists are the Americans. We do not have to differentiate between military and civilian. As far as we are concerned, they are all targets."

The sincerity of bin Laden's words would soon be put to the test. He and al-Zawahiri would prove that they were deadly serious.

Simultaneous Attacks

As the first official joint effort of bin Laden and al-Zawahiri's new group, the two leaders began to plan a devastating attack against American interests. This one would involve simultaneous bombing attacks upon the U.S. Embassies in Nairobi, Kenya, and Dar es Salaam, Tanzania. Several days before the bombings, a Cairo

The shattered and burned-out wreckage of the United States Embassy in Dar es Salaam, Tanzania, on August 8, 1998, one day after it was destroyed by a bomb placed in a fuel tanker parked nearby. Almost simultaneously, another car bomb exploded at the U.S. Embassy in Nairobi, Kenya. The two attacks resulted in the deaths of 231 people, including 12 Americans.

LIBRARY
EDWARD LITTLE HIGH SCHOOL

newspaper received a fax from al-Zawahiri. According to CNN.com, it stated, "We should like to inform the Americans that, in short, their message has been received and that they should read carefully the reply that will, with God's help, be written in the language that they understand."

On the morning of August 7, 1998, the car bombs went off, just as planned. Although 500 miles apart, the explosions occurred at almost exactly the same time. In Nairobi, the embassy building toppled, falling onto streets full of commuter buses, cars, and trucks. In Dar es Salaam, a bomb placed in a fuel tanker exploded in the parking lot of the embassy, destroying two-thirds of the building. Overall, 231 people were killed and 5,000 wounded. For every American killed, roughly 20 Africans (many of them Muslim) died. Four followers of Osama bin Laden and al-Zawahiri were convicted of these crimes in May 2001. More are awaiting trial. In 1999, al-Zawahiri and bin Laden were both indicted by a federal grand jury in New York for their role in these bombings.

September 11, 2001

The carefully coordinated and synchronized East African embassy bombings, horrific as they were, would come to be remembered as an eerie prelude to a far more bloody and elaborately choreographed act—the most devastating terrorist attack ever to occur on American soil. Once again, al-Zawahiri and bin Laden would come together to fund, plan, and organize a massive attack against American civilians. Once again, a number of their followers would be selected, trained, and asked to sacrifice their lives in order to wage war against the so-called enemies of Islam.

Black smoke billows from the north tower of the World Trade Center in New York City following the crash of American Airlines Flight 11 into its side on the morning of September 11, 2001. Eighteen minutes later, United Airlines Flight 175 crashed into the south tower of the World Trade Center at 9:03 AM. Both planes were hijacked and deliberately flown into the towers by Al Qaeda terrorists, led by Mohammed Atta, a member of Egyptian Islamic Jihad. By 10:29 AM, both towers had collapsed, killing almost 3,000 within and near the towers.

And once again, their plan would be executed almost flawlessly. The nineteen hijackers, led by Mohammed Atta, an Egyptian Islamic Jihad member, came to the United States months before September 11, lived in quiet suburban communities, and meticulously prepared their attack. While some attended flight

An airplane hijacked by members of Al Qaeda crashed into the Pentagon, the Department of Defense's headquarters outside Washington, D.C., on September 11, 2001, less than an hour after the north tower of the World Trade Center was attacked. The deliberate crashing of American Airlines Flight 77 into the Pentagon resulted in the deaths of 125 Defense Department employees, 55 airplane passengers, 4 flight attendants, and 2 pilots.

schools, others carefully observed airports and jets, studying cockpits and security procedures at boarding gates. They even took several flights as practice runs.

By al-Zawahiri and bin Laden's grisly standards, the attacks against the United States on September 11, 2001, were a stunning success. The nineteen hijackers, armed with box cutters and knives

Bin Laden Speaks

Following the September 11 attacks, as America began to strike its first targets in Afghanistan as part of Operation Enduring Freedom (a military action, designed to root out and destroy the Al Qaeda terrorist network, that began on October 7, 2001), a videotape of Osama bin Laden was delivered to the Kabul, Afghanistan, office of Al Jazeera, an independent Middle Eastern cable news network. Soon after, it was released to the public. In it, al-Zawahiri is seen sitting next to bin Laden who admits responsibility for the attacks. His words express a cold-blooded analysis of the events that sent chills up many Americans' spines:

"We calculated in advance the number of casualties from the enemy, who would be killed based on the position of the tower. We calculated that the floors that would be hit would be three or four floors. I was the most optimistic of them all due to my experience in this field. I was thinking that the fires from the gas in the plane would melt the iron structure of the building and collapse the area where the plane hit and all the floors above it only. This was all that we had hoped for."

smuggled aboard in their carry-on bags, gained control of four airliners carrying a total of 246 passengers. Some of the hijackers had received just enough flight training to be able to take the controls of the planes and fly them to their intended targets. In essence, the planes were turned into bombs and flown into symbols of American pride, wealth, and power. Two plowed into the World Trade Center towers in New York City. One struck the Pentagon in Arlington, Virginia, (just outside Washington, D.C.). The fourth, perhaps on a collision course with the White House or U.S. Capitol, crashed in a Pennsylvania field while its passengers struggled with the hijackers.

And, as the world watched in horror, the towers fell, killing almost 3,000 trapped workers and rescuers instantly—a nightmarish image of unimaginable cruelty, suffering, and loss that will be seared in our memories forever.

An Uneasy Quiet

The whereabouts of al-Zawahiri and bin Laden were still unknown in the fall of 2002. In the early days of Operation Enduring Freedom, rumors circulated regularly that bin Laden had been killed in a bomb attack or had died of kidney failure or cancer. The growing consensus, however, is that both he and al-Zawahiri are still alive. While the two leaders have been known to separate occasionally in order to hide, official reports state that al-Zawahiri's routine is to stay close to bin Laden most of the time. Together they seem to be trying to reorganize Al Qaeda and the associated Jihad groups. This idea fills many people around the world with a great sense of unease. It is clear that these two men will not stop plotting to murder Americans as long as they remain alive and free.

Conclusion

Though on the run and under attack, bin Laden and al-Zawahiri still lead a terrorist network that some believe contains more than 100,000 militants stationed around the world, as well as command cells in up to fifty countries. Perhaps most troubling, some U.S. intelligence officials believe that 5,000 people currently living in the United States may have ties to the Al Qaeda terrorist network. Many government officials do not wonder if these Islamic terrorists will strike again—but when.

Al-Zawahiri's influence on bin Laden has been immense. Many intelligence experts believe that it was he who first encouraged bin Laden to take up a global struggle against the perceived enemies of Islam. Before meeting al-Zawahiri, the wealthy bin Laden was mainly interested in providing funding for the Afghan resistance to the Soviet invasion. Al-Zawahiri may have been the one to make him think bigger. He is generally credited with making bin Laden "more radical, more anti-American, and more violent," according to Peter Bergen, author of *Holy War, Inc.* Even more troubling, most investigators believe he is smarter, more dangerous, more knowledgeable, and more experienced than bin Laden.

Having emerged as the second highest-ranking leader of the Al Qaeda terrorist network, which now includes Egyptian Islamic Jihad, al-Zawahiri would seem to be the most likely successor to bin Laden. Given al-Zawahiri's reputation for superior intelligence,

Osama bin Laden *(right)* and Ayman al-Zawahiri speak from an undisclosed location in a video broadcast on April 17, 2002, by the London-based Middle East Broadcasting Corporation. In the video, bin Laden celebrates the major blow the September 11 attacks dealt to the U.S. economy and the ongoing psychological harm inflicted on American workers. The tape also includes images of Al Qaeda fighters killed by American bombs dropped in Afghanistan, old statements from bin Laden and his aides, and images of the falling World Trade Center towers.

skill, and ruthlessness, this is a profoundly unsettling notion. As long as he remains free to fund, organize, instruct, and inspire the radical Islamists who are drawn to him, the world's citizens must exist in an agony of uncertainty, wondering when they will be visited by the next deadly explosion of terror.

Glossary

Al Qaeda An Islamic extremist group lead by Osama bin Laden. The name is Arabic for "the foundation" or "the base."

amnesty A general pardon that is usually given to political prisoners.

assassinate To murder (usually a prominent person) by surprise attack for political reasons.

evacuate To withdraw from or vacate a place or an area, especially as a protective measure.

fatwa An Islamic religious statement or command, usually issued by a holy or spiritual leader.

in absentia Something that concerns you that occurs in your absence.

indictment A written statement charging a party with the commission of a crime or another offense, drawn up by a prosecuting attorney. The indictment is ruled upon by a grand jury who determines if the charges are valid and if the case should proceed to trial.

jihad An internal and external struggle to follow the ways of Islam and to protect the faith; often interpreted as a "holy war" against unbelievers.

jurisdiction The territorial range of authority or control.

Koran (Qur'an) A book of sacred writings believed by Muslims to be the revelations of Allah (God) to his prophet Muhammad through the angel Gabriel.

For More Information

The Center for Defense Information
1779 Massachusetts Avenue NW
Washington, DC 20036-2109
(202) 332-0600
Web site: http://www.cdi.org

Central Intelligence Agency (CIA)
Office of Public Affairs
Washington, DC 20505
(703) 482-0623
Web site: http://www.cia.gov

Council on American-Islamic Relations (CAIR)
453 New Jersey Avenue SE
Washington, DC 20003-4034
(202) 488-8787
Web site: http://www.cair-net.org

Federal Bureau of Investigation (FBI)
J. Edgar Hoover Building
935 Pennsylvania Avenue NW
Washington, DC 20535-0001
(202) 324-3000
Web site: http://www.fbi.gov

For More Information

Federation of American Scientists (FAS)
Intelligence Resource Program
1717 K Street NW, Suite 209
Washington, DC 20036
(202) 454-4691
Web site: http://www.fas.org/irp/index.html

Institute of Islamic Information and Education
P.O. Box 41129
Chicago, IL 60641-0129
(773) 777-7443
Web site: http://www.iiie.net

National Security Agency (NSA)
Public Affairs Office
9800 Savage Road
Fort George G. Meade, MD 20755-6779
(301) 688-6524
Web site: http://www.nsa.gov

National Security Institute (NSI)
116 Main Street, Suite 200
Medway, MA 02053
(508) 533-9099
Web site: http://nsi.org

Terrorist Group Profiles
Dudley Knox Library
Naval Post Graduate School
411 Dyer Road
Monterey, CA 93943
Web site: http://library.nps.navy.mil/home/tgp/tgpndx.htm

Web Sites

Due to the changing nature of Internet links, the Rosen Publishing Group, Inc., has developed an online list of Web sites related to the subject of this book. This site is updated regularly. Please use this link to access the list:

http://www.rosenlinks.com/iwmito/egij/

For Further Reading

Gaines, Ann. *Terrorism*. Broomall, PA: Chelsea House
　　Publications, 1998.

Gordon, Matthew S. *Islam*. New York: Facts on File, 1991.

Hamilton, Josh. *Behind the Terror*. Minneapolis: Abdo and
　　Daughters, 2002.

Holliday, Laurel. *Why Do They Hate Me?* Minneapolis: Econo-Clad
　　Books, 2000.

Hurley, Jennifer, ed. *Islam*. San Diego: Greenhaven Press, 2000.

Khan, Rukhsana. *Muslim Child: Understanding Islam through
　　Stories and Poems*. Morton Grove, IL: Albert Whitman and
　　Co., 2002.

Louis, Nancy. *Ground Zero*. Minneapolis: Abdo and
　　Daughters, 2002.

Louis, Nancy. *Heroes of the Day*. Minneapolis: Abdo and
　　Daughters, 2002.

Louis, Nancy. *United We Stand*. Minneapolis: Abdo and
　　Daughters, 2002.

Markovitz, Hal. *Terrorism*. Broomall, PA: Chelsea House
　　Publications, 2002.

Shields, Charles. *The World Trade Center Bombing*. Broomall,
　　PA: Chelsea House Publications, 2001.

Stewart, Gail. *Terrorism*. Farmington Hills, MI: Kidhaven
　　Press, 2002.

Wells, Donna Koren, and Bruce Morris. *Live Aware, Not in Fear: The 411 After 911: A Book for Teens*. Deerfield Beach, FL: Health Communications, Inc., 2002.

Wormser, Richard. *American Islam: Growing Up Muslim in America*. New York: Walker, 1994.

Bibliography

Associated Press. "5,000 in U.S. May Have al-Qaida Ties." NYTimes.com. July 11, 2002. Retrieved July 11, 2002 (http://www.nytimes.com/aponline/national/AP-Attacks-Terror-Network.html).

"At Least 60 Dead in Egypt Tourist Attack." CNN.com. November 17, 1997. Retrieved May 10, 2002 (http://www.cnn.com/WORLD/9711/17/egypt.attack.update2/).

Bin Laden, Osama. "Jihad Against Jews and Crusaders World Islamic Front Statement." Federation of American Scientists. February 23, 1998. Retrieved May 16, 2002 (http://www.fas.org/irp/world/para/docs/980223-fatwa.htm).

Blanche, Ed. "Ayman Al-Zawahiri: Attention Turns to the Other Prime Suspect." Jane's International Review. October 3, 2001. Retrieved May 15, 2002 (http://www.janes.com/security/international_security/news/jir/jir/011003_1_n.shtml).

Bush, President George W. "Transcript of President Bush's Address." CNN.com. September 21, 2001. Retrieved May 10, 2002 (http://www.cnn.com/2001/US/09/20/gen.bush.transcript/).

"Bush Denounces Muslim Harassment." CNN.com. September 17, 2001. Retrieved May 2002 (http://www.cnn.com/2001/us/09/17/gen.hate.crimes./).

"Egyptian Physician with a $5 Million Price on his Head." CNN.com. 2001. Retrieved May 10, 2002 (http://www.cnn.com/CNN/Programs/people/shows/zawahiri/profile.html).

Emerson, Steven. *American Jihad: The Terrorists Living Among Us*. New York: Simon and Schuster, 2002.

Esposito, John. *Unholy War: Terror in the Name of Islam*. New York: Oxford University Press, 2002.

Hiel, Betsy. "Egyptian Islamic Jihad Linked to bin Laden." Pittsburgh Live.com. September 15, 2001. Retrieved May 8, 2002 (http://www.pittsburghlive.com/x/tribune-review/columnists/hiel/s_3028.html).

Kepel, Gilles. *Jihad: The Trail of Political Islam*. Cambridge, MA: Harvard University Press, 2002.

Landau, Elaine. *Osama bin Laden: A War Against the West*. Brookfield, CT: Twenty-First Century Books, 2002.

Marsh, Carole. *The Day that Was Different: September 11, 2001: When Terrorists Attacked America*. Peachtree City, GA: Gallopade International, 2001.

Mylroie, Laurie. "The World Trade Center Bomb: Who Is Ramzi Yousef? And Why It Matters." The National Interest. 1996. Retrieved June 2002 (http://www.fas.org/irp/world/iraq/956-tni.htm).

Nelan, Bruce W. "The Dark Side of Islam." Time.com. October 4, 1993. Retrieved May 10, 2002 (http://www.time.com/nation/printout/0,8816,174514,00.html).

"Profile: bin Laden's Right Hand Man." BBC News.com. September 24, 2001. Retrieved May 10, 2002 (http://news.bbc.co.uk/hi/english/world/middle_east/newsid_1560000/1560834.stm).

Raafat, Amir. "The World's Second Most Wanted Man." The Star. November 22, 2001. Retrieved May 10, 2002 (http://www.fas/org/irp/world/para/ayman.htm).

Bibliography

Rashid, Ahmed. *Jihad: The Rise of Militant Islam in Central Asia*. New Haven, CT: Yale University Press, 2002.

Spencer, William. *Islamic Fundamentalism and the Modern World*. Brookfield, CT: Millbrook Press, 1995.

"What Happened at Luxor?" BBC News.com. November 19, 1997. Retrieved May 10, 2002 (http://news6.thdo.bbc.co.ul/hi/english/world/newsid_32000/32722.stm).

"Who Are Islamic Jihad?" BBC News. December 3, 2001. Retrieved May 10, 2002 (http://news.bbc.co.uk/hi/english/in_depth/middle_east/2001/israel_and_the_palestinians/profiles/newsid_1658000/1658443.stm).

Williams, Dave. "The Bombing of the World Trade Center in New York City." Interpol/International Police Crime Review. Retrieved May 10, 2002 (http://www.interpol.int/Public/Publications/ICPR/ICPR469_3.asp).

Wolf, Buck. "Memories of the First Trade Center Attack." ABC News.com. September 11, 2001. Retrieved May 10, 2002 (http://abcnews.go.com/sections/us/DailyNews/wtcbombings1993account010911.html).

Index

About the Author

Tamra Orr is the author of a dozen books for families, including *Native American Medicine*, *Korean-Americans*, and *The Parent's Guide to Homeschooling*. She is mom to four children, wife to Joseph, and a full-time freelance writer living in Portland, Oregon.

Photo Credits

Cover, p. 35 © Corbis; pp. 1, 52 © AP/Wide World Photos; p. 5 © Ron Edmonds/AP/Wide World Photos; p. 6 © Plinio Lepri/AP/Wide World Photos; pp. 10–11 © Claro/TimePix; p. 13 © TimePix; p. 15 © Hulton/Archive/Getty Images; pp. 21, 22–23 © Kevin Fleming/Corbis; p. 27 © Marty Lederhandler/Corbis; p. 31 © Mike Segar/Corbis; p. 38 © B. K. Bangash/AP/Wide World Photos; p. 41 © Dimitri Messinis/AP/Wide World Photos; pp. 44–45 © Brennan Linsley/AP/Wide World Photos; p. 47 © Chao Soi Cheong/AP/Wide World Photos; p. 48 © Steve Helber/AP/Wide World Photos.

Series Design and Layout

Nelson Sá